PAT TUNG'S
Fried Ice Cream
& Other Gourmet Delights

Pat Tung

illustrated by Sarah Dresing

Published by Pat Tung's International Gourmet, Inc.
Rocky River, Ohio

This book is dedicated to my family and especially to my parents-in-law. My special thanks go to all the contributors of recipes, and to Janet Long, Julia Ball, Jane Young, Gayle Cerrito, Helene Srawley, Paul Ferrara, David Cole, Christina and Hwa-min Hsu, and Pandemonium.

Edited by Kendra Crossen

Photographs by Ed Nano/Tableware courtesy of Mrs. David T. Morgenthaler

Library of Congress Catalog Card Number: 84-91413
ISBN: 0-9614469-0-0

First Printing, May 1985

Printed in the United States of America
Wimmer Brothers Books
P.O. Box 18408
Memphis, TN 38118
"Cookbooks of Distinction" ™

Contents

Introduction: A Culinary Miracle™   7

1
All About Frying with Super Batter Mix   13

2
Jiffy Basics for Everyday Enjoyment   27

Appetizers: Shrimp Tempura, 28 Appetizing Oysters, 29 Crisp Clams, 30 Fried Potato Skins, 31 Chicken Lollipops, 32

Main Dishes: Scrumptious Chicken Breasts, 33 Chicken Supernuggets, 34 Terrific Teriyaki, 35 A Fifteen-Minute Complete Meal Plan, 36 Fantastic Fish, 37 Pork Tenderloin, 38 Precious Veal, 39

Vegetables: Asparagus, 40 Broccoli, 40 Cauliflower, 40 Eggplant, 40 Green Beans, 40 Mushrooms, 40 Best-Ever Onion Rings, 41 Potatoes, 41 Spinach, 42 Tomatoes, 42 Yams, 42 Zucchini, 42

Desserts: Yummy Bananas, 43 Banana Supreme, 44 Apples Americana, 45 Peachy Peaches, 46 Nectarine Nibbler, 47 Fried Ice-Cream Sandwiches, 47

3
Simple, Elegant Delectables for Special Occasions

49

Appetizers: Glorious Cheese, 50 Aristocratic Artichoke Hearts, 51 Sensational Cheesy Mushrooms, 52 Zestful Zucchini Blossoms, 53 Tasty Turkey Cheese Rolls, 54

Main Dishes: Coconut Scampi, 55 Super Scallops, 56 Sweet-Sour Chicken or Pork, 56 Meat Balls, 58 Incredible Crepes, 59 Chiles Rellenos de Queso, 60

Vegetables: Splendid Zucchini Stuffed with Caviar, 61 Mouth-Watering Soufflé, 62 Fried Chèvre Cheese on Salad, 63 Vegetable Trios, 64

Desserts: Fabulous Fried Strawberries or Pineapple, 65 Flaming Banana, 66 Party Pound Cake, 67 Fried Ice Cream in Cake, 69 Waffle Wonders, 70 Fried Ice Cream in Cornflakes, 71 Icy Rice Krispies, 72 Fried Ice Cream in Crepes, 73 Fried Ice Cream in Almond Paste, 74

4

Other Serving Ideas 77

Breakfast: Fried Waffles, 78   Crispy English Muffins, 78   Fried Bread, 79

Brunch: Stuffed French Toast, 80

Lunch: Deep-Fried Hot Dogs, 81   Mashed Potato and Tuna Patties, 82

Snack: Sunflower Seed Fritters, 82

Precooked Foods: Cold-Cut Meat Roll, 83   Roast Beef with Smoked Clams, 83

Leftovers: Fried Pizza, 83   Meat and Poultry, 83

Summertime Quickies: Seafood Kabobs, 84   Chicken and Vegetable Kabobs, 85

Wintertime Fun: Fish and Chicken Fry Party, 86

5

Sauces and Dips 89

Tangy Apricot Sauce, 90 Orange-Honey Sauce, 90 Butterscotch Syrup, 90 Tomato Salsa, 91 Oriental Soy-Sherry Dip, 91 Oriental Soy-Vinegar Dip, 91 Hot and Spicy Mustard Dip, 92 Hot and Sweet Mustard Dip, 92 Creamy Mustard Dip, 92 Artichoke Blue-Cheese Dip, 93 Mustard Vinaigrette Dressing, 93 Yogurt Mustard Dip or Dressing, 93

Introduction:
A Culinary Miracle™

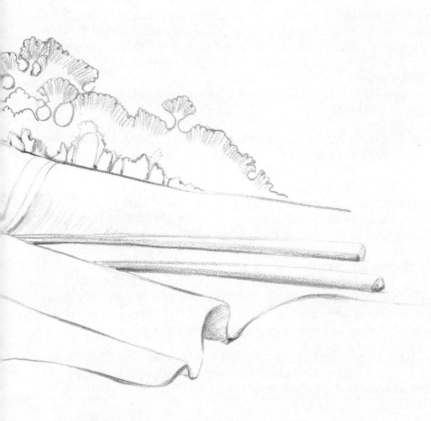

Introduction: A Culinary Miracle™

As a cooking school teacher, one of my biggest challenges has been to create special recipes to meet the specific expectations of my gourmet students. My Super Batter Mix™ was one such creation.

My quest for an ideal batter began years ago when students asked me how to make a really good batter for deep-frying. Many expressed their disappointment with existing commercial products. These were either too floury, not crisp enough, or too thick, or they contained MSG, salt, preservatives, additives, or other unwanted ingredients. Some students had tried cookbook recipes but complained that the batter turned out to be too lumpy, would not stick to the food, or absorbed too much oil, making the food unpleasantly greasy. Some batter simply failed to create a nicely finished product; when the food got cold, the batter just flattened and softened. Moreover, most batter recipes contained eggs, which are a dietary restriction for many people.

The Super Batter Mix that I created is free of all the above defects and guarantees satisfactory results. It makes a light, crisp golden-brown coating with a smooth, shiny appearance, encasing the moist, succulent food inside, whether it is meat, poultry, fish, vegetable, or fruit. Just the sight of food made with Super Batter Mix will make your mouth water. The taste is absolutely delicious. It is a true delight, as it provides the perfect combination of flavor, color, and texture.

More important, Super Batter Mix has been created to have the following desirable features:

Simplicity: By just adding water and oil, you can mix up the batter in a jiffy. Leftover batter can be covered, refrigerated, and reused within a few days. The batter always sticks to the food, and there is no special procedure for applying it. What used to be a troublesome cooking task now becomes a simple and straightforward operation. Ninety-eight percent of the recipes in this book take only three to four minutes to fry a batch. As for cooking utensils, a deep-fryer is not a must. A wok, a skillet, a fry-daddy, an electric fondue set, or even a regular saucepan will do—as long as it can be heated up to 375°-400°F. (If you use a skillet, you can cover the unused burners with upside-down aluminum pie plates to avoid oil splatters. Placing foil, tucked tight, on the adjacent counters will also reduce cleaning time afterward.)

Quality: Super Batter Mix forms a feather-light, crisp, nongreasy coating. It retains crispness for a relatively long time. It does not absorb food odor, so the oil you used to fry fish with can be used later for frying fruits.

Healthfulness: Super Batter Mix contains no eggs, MSG, preservatives, or additives and no salt added. When people think of batter-frying, they usually associate it with deep fat and greasiness. This is not necessarily the case when you use Super Batter Mix. I advocate the method of *shallow-frying*—that is, you use less oil (¾ to 2½ inches in depth) to brown one side of the food, while basting the side that is above the oil level with a spoon; you then turn it over to brown the other side. If food is sliced thin or if it will not leak out of the coating, then basting is not necessary. Placing fried food on a rack above a pan before serving or while warming is another grease-eliminating step this book recommends.

Versatility: Super Batter Mix has almost endless uses and will easily coat many different items from all four food groups, from tasty appetizers to tantalizing desserts, including everyone's favorite fruits and ice cream. Food can be prefried and frozen or refrigerated for later use. It can then be refried or warmed in the oven.

I started to market Super Batter Mix in the Cleveland area in November 1982. It has been greeted with an overwhelmingly enthusiastic response. The only complaint I received was that my batter tasted so good that children would just eat the crust and leave the filling of chicken, fish, or shrimp! The mix has been introduced to thousands of individuals and households, and used by professional chefs and gourmet restaurants as well.

Many chefs have used the batter in their own creative ways and thus added new ideas to the culinary field. When I do demonstrations in public and on television, people in the audience often volunteer suggestions and novel applications for my products, and I am grateful for these inspirations.

Widely hailed as the best of its kind, Super Batter Mix is highly regarded by those who have had a chance to use it. People use it on a regular basis, for everyday meals, for parties, and even on fishing and camping trips. Many have sent my products to their relatives and friends throughout the country.

This book includes both recipes that I developed myself and ideas contributed by professional chefs. There are enough to cover full-course meals, from appetizer to dessert.

In conclusion, I totally agree with the saying I once read in an advertisement: "It's the batter that matters." I call my Super Batter Mix a culinary miracle, for it can help turn any cook into a gourmet chef instantly. It is my sincere hope that this book and its recipes will bring some joy and excitement to those with a discriminating taste.

9

COMMENTS ABOUT SUPER BATTER MIX:

"Feather light, never-fail batter mix with a multitude of uses. I wouldn't be without it."

Russ Vernon
President, West Point Market
Akron, Ohio

"Pat has created a batter-fried feast. Her recipes transcend oriental tempura as I know it."

Lindsay J. Morgenthaler
Cleveland, Ohio

"Your batter is precious and delicious. My family loved it."

Bunny Adelman
Cookworld
New York, New York

"The taste is perfect!"

**Kazuko Yano,
Naperville, Illinois**

"We have tried so many coating products, but until we had yours nothing was satisfactory. All I can say is now we are hooked on a fantastic product . . . Thank you for developing such a wonderful item!"

**Judy G. Cirelly
Geneva, Ohio**

"We loved it, especially my son, who picked all the batter off the shrimp and ate just the batter!"

**Cynthia Satterlee
Chicago, Illinois**

"Your batter is fantastic! The lightest, crispiest coating we'd ever tasted! I have to tell you I'll never again search for a recipe or batter mix for fish for my family. I told a friend of mine, and she took some home with her to another state. She wrote later that her family also has adopted your mix as their very favorite and will never use another."

**Babs Hajdusiewicz
Rocky River, Ohio**

1

All About Frying with Super Batter Mix

USES

The uses of Super Batter Mix are endless. Here is a list of foods I recommend.

MILK AND DAIRY PRODUCTS

Hard Cheeses
Cheddar
Colby
Edam
Fontina
Goat cheese
Gruyère
Montrachet
Monterey Jack
Mozzarella
Swiss

Cheese Stuffings
Boursin
Cheddar, shredded
Cream cheese
Crumbled blue cheese
Mozzarella, shredded

Ice Cream
Ice-cream sandwiches
Party ice-cream slices
Any flavor of ice cream

MEAT, POULTRY, AND SEAFOOD

Beef
Veal
Pork: chops, tenderloin, loin
Ham
Cold cuts
Chicken: boneless breast, thigh, drumstick, drumettes, wings
Turkey

Duck
Squab
Eggs
Fish fillets
Smelts
Shrimp
Scampi
Prawns
Lobster
King crab legs
Soft-shell crab
Crab claws
Crab sticks or seafood sticks
Clams: cherrystone, littleneck, top neck, ocean
Oysters: smoked, freshwater
Mussels
Scallops: bay, sea
Octopus
Squid (calamari)
Sepia
Abalone
Conch

VEGETABLES

Artichoke hearts
Asparagus
Avocado
Broccoli
Carrots
Cauliflower
Celery
Corn
Cucumber
Eggplant
Green and yellow beans
Hearts of palm
Lotus root
Mushrooms: fresh, Shiitake, Chinese dried

Okra
Onion: any variety
Parsley: regular, curly
Pepper: green, sweet red, yellow (mildly hot), chilies
Potato
Potato skins
Snow peas
Spinach
Yams or sweet potatoes
Yellow squash
Zucchini: blossoms, squash

FRUITS AND DESSERTS

Apple
Banana
Nectarine
Peach
Pineapple
Strawberry
Tomato
Pound cake

BREAD AND CEREAL

Bread: any kind
English muffin
Waffles

PREPARED FOODS

Burritos
Croquettes
Hot dogs
Sauerkraut balls
Stuffed cabbage
Leftover meat
Precooked meat

. . . And many more!

PREPARING THE BATTER

Mix a 5½-ounce packet of Super Batter Mix (approximately 1 cup) with ¾ cup (6 ounces) cold water and 1 tablespoon oil (corn, peanut, or vegetable).

The prepared batter will have a consistency like that of pancake batter. If you lift it up with a fork, it should drip down in a string. If the batter seems too thick, add a few drops of water. To thin batter, always adjust the amount of water a little at a time.

QUESTIONS AND ANSWERS

Q. Why batter-fry food? Why not just fry directly, without batter?

A. In batter-frying, food is coated with a batter, then fried in hot oil. Through the indirect heat, the food gets cooked without changing its texture, and the natural flavor and moisture are retained within a crisp outer coating. Above all, the batter adds a wonderful taste to the food. Batter-frying appears in many cuisines of the world. Perhaps the best-known dish is the Japanese specialty called tempura.

Q. How much food can one packet of Super Batter Mix coat?

A. The label of the 5½-ounce packet says that the contents will coat *at least* one pound of food. Actually, that is a rather conservative statement in most cases. It all depends on the food item, its size and shape, how much batter you use, and how much you waste. One packet can coat eight pieces of fish or forty to fifty slices of zucchini or banana. After coating food, be sure to let the batter drip off as much as possible. The result will be a very light, crisp coating with a short cooking time, and you will also have more batter to coat more food.

Q. Can I use only a portion of a Super Batter Mix packet?

A. Certainly. If you are cooking for two, use half a 5½-ounce packet—that is, 2¾ ounces. Or you may measure ½ cup of the mix, then add 6 tablespoons (3 ounces) water and ½ tablespoon (1½ teaspoons) oil. For an even smaller portion, mix ¼ cup mix with 3 tablespoons water and ¾ teaspoons oil.

Q. Can the batter be reused? How long does it last?

A. Leftover batter can be reused if you keep the unused portion covered and refrigerated. To save the time and effort of transferring the leftover mix from one utensil to another, mix the batter in a container or mixing bowl with a lid. A plastic container that once contained frozen whipped topping is good. The batter will last three to four days refrigerated. It is best to use leftover batter the next day, as refrigerated batter tends to dry out. If this seems to have happened to your batter, add a few drops of water and stir well. To serve a family of four, many of my customers fry chicken one night and have fried fish the second night—thus, one 5½-ounce packet of Super Batter Mix will take care of two meals.

Q. What is the difference in the varieties of Super Batter Mix?

A. The *All Purpose* Super Batter Mix is the basic type and can be used for food ranging from appetizers to desserts. You may add salt, spices, or sugar to it, depending on the usage. The *Seasoned* Super Batter Mix contains spices and herbs. It can be used for anything except desserts. The *Spicy* Super Batter Mix is mildly hot. It contains cayenne pepper and other spices. It can be used for anything except desserts.

Q. Can I add salt and spices to the batter?

A. Certainly. If you wish, add ½ to 1 teaspoon salt and a small amount of spices or seasonings to Super Batter Mix before adding oil or water. You may also add a small amount of sesame seeds, bread crumbs, or chopped green onion to the batter.

Q. Will the batter stick to moist and wet food?

A. Not every piece. With moist and wet food, such as pineapple or strawberries, dust the item in a mixture of equal parts flour and cornstarch to absorb the moisture. Then dip in the batter and fry.

Q. What type of oil should I use?

A. I recommend polyunsaturated varieties such as corn, peanut, or vegetable oil. Corn and peanut oil can sustain high temperatures without smoking easily. Many commercial operations use liquid shortening.

Q. How much oil do I need to use?

A. It depends on the cooking utensil you are using, the amount of food you plan to cook, and the thickness of the food. The wider the utensil, the more oil it takes. Normally, in deep-frying, which is ideal for batter-frying, food is completely immersed in oil. I suggest *shallow-frying,* which uses considerably less oil. I use 1½-2 cups oil in a wok for an average amount of food. A depth of oil ranging from ¾ to 2½ inches (depending on the thickness of the food used) is enough to make most food float to the surface when done. You help compensate for the shallowness of the oil by basting cooking oil over the portion of food above the oil level with a long-handled spoon (never use a baster!). With experience, you may use less oil.

Q. Do I need a deep-fry or candy thermometer to test the oil?

A. It's not necessary, but if you have one, use it. The temperature should be 350°-375°F. (medium high) for deep-frying. Often, however, experience is the best guide. To test whether or not the oil is ready for frying, put a drop of batter into the oil (never use water!). The oil is ready to use if the batter immediately sizzles and rises to the surface. Do not fry too many pieces of food at a time, for that will cause the temperature of the oil to drop and then the food will absorb the oil and become greasy. To deep-fry food such as ice cream or cheese, you should raise the temperature in order to shorten the cooking time. For ready-to-eat foods such as fruit, you can set the temperature at 375°-400°F.

Q. Can I reuse the oil?

A. For health reasons, it's not a good idea to use and reuse oil repeatedly in frying. In order to avoid waste, I suggest you use less oil each time. I use oil twice at the most, but if the oil turns dark even after one use, I discard it. If oil is to be reused, be sure to strain it when cool through a paper towel or drip coffee filter placed in a funnel, sieve, or wire strainer.

Q. How do you make fried food nongreasy?

A. Any fried food absorbs a certain amount of oil. Some will do so only on the surface and others all the way through. To reduce oil to a minimum, try the following techniques.

1. Control the temperature. If the oil is not hot enough to seal the food, the food ends up sitting in lukewarm oil, absorbing the oil instead of frying properly. Moreover, the batter will separate from the food if the oil is not hot enough. The food will not only take longer to cook, but will also be soggy and greasy. The ideal temperature is 375°F. (medium high). If the temperature is too high, the coating gets burnt while the inside is half-cooked.

2. Use a strainer or a long-handled slotted spoon to remove the food, drain the oil off, and help remove batter crumbs from the oil before frying a new batch. (The batter crumbs make delicious munchies!)

3. Place fried food on a rack above a foil-lined pan (do not pile fried items close together!) to let excess oil drip off. (Use a tempura rack if you have one.) The purpose is not only to let the oil drip down, but also to let air circulate around the food so that it will stay crisp. If you have to complete the frying in several batches, you may place the food on the rack over a pan in a warm oven. You will notice that the oil drips on the foil in the pan. Blot the food with a paper towel before serving.

4. You may also reverse this procedure. Place the food on paper toweling after cooking to blot the oil, then place it immediately on a rack over a foil-lined pan. *Note:* To save paper towels, place a few layers of brown bags or newspaper underneath paper towels if the food is to be eaten right away.

21

Q. Why should I drain fried foods on a rack over a foil-lined pan? Can't I just use paper towels alone?

A. When fried food is drained on paper towels, one side of the food tends to get soft because of the moisture produced by the trapped heat. By using a rack, you can keep the air circulating around the freshly fried items, so that they remain crisp all around while they cool. In addition, you allow excess oil to drain through. (However, on a very humid day, the moisture in the air will tend to soften fried foods.) By using a rack, you avoid eating the grease that often results from reheating fried foods (such as doggie-bag items) directly on a cookie sheet or piece of foil. Lining your pan with foil, which can be easily disposed of, eliminates the cleaning of a greasy pan afterward.

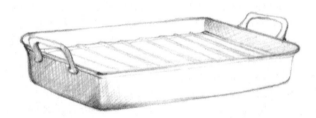

Q. Can I freeze or refrigerate batter-fried food?

A. Yes. Everyone knows that freshly fried food tastes the best. However, it may be easier for busy people to do all of the cooking at once, then wait until the food cools to room temperature before refrigerating or freezing it for later use.

Q. How do I warm up frozen or cold batter-fried food?

A. Refrying the food in hot oil at medium-high (375°F) temperature is the quickest way and also ensures crispness. A suggestion: During the initial frying, remove the food when it is fully cooked but only lightly browned, so that the second frying will result in a golden-brown color and a crisp texture. Warming food in the oven (375°-400°F.) is another alternative. Place the food on a rack over a foil-lined pan. Warm it for 15-20 minutes, depending on the type of food and its size. Turn it once after 8-10 minutes.

Q. What type of cooking utensils should I use?

A. Any kind of utensil will do—a deep-fryer, a wok, a skillet, an electric fondue, a fry-daddy, or, as a last resort, a regular saucepan. Use tongs, chopsticks, or a slotted spoon to transfer food from batter to oil. A slotted spoon is especially helpful with items that are hard to pick up, such as crepes and ice-cream slices. Use a long-handled spoon for basting when shallow-frying.

Q. What kind of utensil should I mix the batter with?

A. It doesn't matter. I use a wire whisk or chopsticks to blend the batter. You can use a mixer if you prefer.

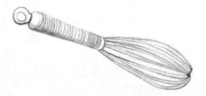

Q. Why does the batter get thinner toward the end?

A. The consistency of the batter should stay the same throughout its use. If you do not drain the food and pat it dry before coating, you will inadvertently add water to the batter, thus making it thinner.

Q. My kids love bread crumbs. Can I double-coat foods?

A. Definitely. To add interest and texture and variety, create your own second coating. Dip food in Super Batter Mix, then coat with bread crumbs, crushed croutons, ground corn flakes, coconut flakes, chopped nuts (almonds, walnuts, pecans, macadamia, etc.) sesame seeds, etc.

Q. How can I vary the taste of battered foods?

A. By using your favorite recipes of various dips, sauces, and garnishes, you will be able to create an international feast with your creativity. It's fun!

SAFETY TIPS

1. Keep children away from the cooking area when you are deep-frying.
2. Always be sure to turn your stove off (or unplug your appliance) when it is not in use. Allow it to cool before cleaning.
3. Always move the utensil containing hot oil to the rear (inside) burner when cooking is done.
4. Let oil cool before transferring it to a bottle or container. Hot oil will crack a glass bottle and melt a plastic container.
5. Always turn the handle of your cooking utensil to the side, instead of letting it stick out in front of the range, unless it is being attended.
6. Before using an electrical appliance, please read the information on safety precautions that came with the appliance.
7. If you are simultaneously boiling water in a tea kettle and deep-frying, make sure the spout of the kettle is always pointing away from the oil. At best, try not to do these two things at the same time.
8. Do not let an electric cord hang over the edge or touch hot surfaces.
9. Have food and batter conveniently located near the cooking utensils. Be sure to pat moist or wet food dry, or the liquid in the food may splatter. If it starts to splatter, stand back after the food is added to the oil, or cover the oil for a short while.
10. Never use a baster to baste hot oil over food that is above the oil level. Use a long-handled spoon.

2
Jiffy Basics for Everyday Enjoyment

All so easy to prepare,
yet all finger-licking good!

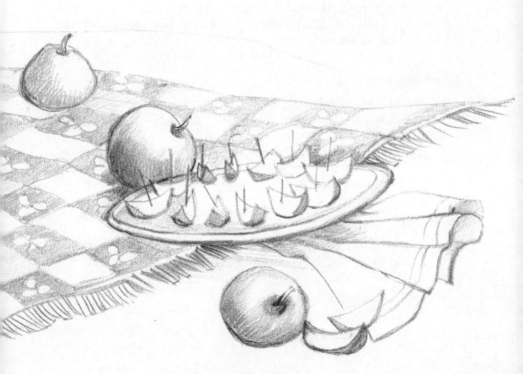

Shrimp Tempura

A classic—succulent shrimp in a light, crisp batter. What a treat!

**1 lb. fresh shrimp (preferably large size) or
  frozen shrimp
Super Batter Mix
oil for deep-frying**

Preparation

1. Shell shrimp, but leave the tails on. Thaw frozen shrimp and drain well.
2. Cut each shrimp open from the back all the way to the inner curve, but do not cut through.
3. Open each shrimp flat into a large piece. Devein, rinse, and pat dry. Pound shrimp with the flat side of a knife.
4. Mix batter.

Cooking

1. Heat oil to medium high (375°F). Dip shrimp into batter, either one at a time or five at a time by holding the ends of the tails. Let excess batter drip off.
2. When oil is ready, drop in five or six shrimp at a time. When one side is brown, turn over. When both sides are golden brown (approximately 3-4 minutes), remove.

To Serve

• Serve with Pat Tung's Gourmet Delight Sweet Sour Sauce or Mustard Dipping Mix.

Appetizing Oysters

Super Batter Mix
1 tbsp. cornstarch
1 tbsp. flour
1 lb. shucked raw oysters (blue point or other
  variety)
oil for deep-frying

Preparation

1. Mix batter.
2. Mix cornstarch and flour in a plate or dish.
3. Rinse oysters and pat dry. Dip in cornstarch and flour mix, then dust off.

Cooking

Heat oil to 375°F. Dip each oyster in batter and deep-fry until golden brown (2-3 minutes).

To Serve

- Serve with Pat Tung's Gourmet Delight Mustard Dipping Sauce, Sweet Sour Sauce or horseradish.

Note: Oysters easily cause splatters during frying. Be prepared!

Crisp Clams

This recipe was inspired by Michael Gale, who is a chef in Honolulu, Hawaii.

> **1 lb. shucked raw cherrystone, top neck, or littleneck
> clams**
> **1 tsp. salt**
> **¼ tsp. pepper**
> **Super Batter Mix**
> **2 tbsp. flour**
> **oil for deep-frying**

Preparation

1. Rinse shucked clams and pat dry. Season with salt and pepper.
2. Mix batter.

Cooking

1. Lightly roll clams in flour, then dust off excess flour.
2. Heat oil to 375°F. Dip each clam in batter and deep-fry until golden brown.

To Serve

- Dip crisp fried clams into Creamy Mustard Dip (see page 92), cocktail sauce, tartar sauce, mayonnaise, or ketchup.

Duane Bubsey's Fried Potato Skins

This is superb as either an appetizer or a main dish. Duane Bubsey is the head chef at Our Gang in Rocky River, Ohio

Super Batter Mix
6 large Idaho potatoes
oil for frying

TOPPINGS
choice of

- **shredded Cheddar cheese**
  real bacon bits
  sour cream
- **chives**
  sour cream

- **guacamole**
  shredded Cheddar cheese
  sour cream
- **fresh cooked asparagus (chopped)**
  Hollandaise on top

Preparation

1. Mix batter. (It may be prepared ahead of time and refrigerated. Before using, stir it again or whip it.)
2. Scrub potatoes clean. Pat dry and cut each potato in half lengthwise.
3. Bake potatoes at 350°F for 45 minutes. Use a knife or spoon to remove pulp, but leave ⅛ to ¼-inch attached to skin. (Or microwave each potato for 4-5 minutes.)

Cooking

Dip potato skins in batter to coat both sides. Let excess batter drip off. Heat oil to 375°F. Fry potato skins with skin side down first. Turn over to hollow side when brown. If shallow-frying, baste with oil. Remove when both sides are brown (approximately 3-4 minutes).

To Serve

- See toppings above.
- To make Chef Duane's Loaded Skins, fill potato skin with chili and top with lots of cheese. Serve with Mexican salsa on the side.
- Or create your own filling!

Chicken Lollipops

A fine appetizer or main dish.

1 lb. (12-15) chicken drumettes
½-1 tsp. salt
¼ tsp. pepper
Super Batter Mix
oil for frying

Preparation

1. Rinse drumettes and pat dry. Sprinkle with salt and pepper, and let stand for 15 minutes in refrigerator.
2. Separate meat from bone on smaller end by making four downward 2-inch cuts all around so that meat is detached.
3. Using the palm of your hand to smooth the detached meat so that it covers the larger end of the drumette, form a lollipop-like ball on one end so that the bone is free of meat.
4. Mix batter.

Cooking

Heat oil to 350°F. Dip chicken in batter and fry until both sides are brown and crispy (approximately 8-10 minutes).

To Serve

- Let lollipops stand on plate with meat side down. Serve with your favorite sauce or Hot and Sweet Mustard Dip (see page 92).
- To serve a large crowd, precook chicken lollipops (by either steaming or boiling) after step 3, cool, dip in batter, and fry till brown.

Scrumptious Chicken Breasts

Sink your teeth into this juicy, plump entrée or sandwich!

4 boneless chicken breast halves
Super Batter Mix
Pat Tung's Gourmet Delight Sesame Seeds
  (optional)
oil for frying

Preparation

1. Rinse chicken breast and pat dry. Slice into two thin pieces by making a horizontal cut starting about 2 inches from the tail end (thin side), or pound chicken with a mallet into even thickness and then cut into two pieces.
2. Season chicken if you wish.
3. Mix batter.

Cooking

Heat oil to 375°F. Dip chicken in batter, roll in sesame seeds (if desired). Deep-fry for 2-2½ minutes. Turn over and fry other side. Remove when both sides are golden brown. Place fried batch on a rack above a pan in a warm oven while frying the rest.

To Serve

• Serve with Pat Tung's Gourmet Delight Sweet Sour Sauce.
• Place fried chicken fillet in a warm toasted sesame roll, adding lettuce, cheese, tomatoes, and onion and pepper rings.
• Sandwich in a French croissant, adding cheese, mushrooms, or onion slices.

Note: By slicing chicken into two equal thicknesses, you ensure an even texture for your eating pleasure. Alternately, you may fry the chicken breasts whole, or cut the thin parts and fry them together, using less time. Fry thicker parts approximately 4-5 minutes.

Chicken Supernuggets

---

4 filleted chicken breast halves
Super Batter Mix
oil for deep-frying

Preparation

1. Cut chicken into nuggets 1½-inches square and ⅜-inch thick.
2. Mix batter.

Cooking

Heat oil to 375°F. Dip chicken in batter and let excess batter drip off. Deep-fry five or six pieces until both sides turn golden brown (approximately 3-4 minutes). Remove chicken nuggets and place on a rack above a baking dish in the oven to keep warm. Continue to deep-fry the rest.

Note: Cooked chicken nuggets, when cooled, may be refrigerated or frozen for future use. To reheat, either deep-fry in 375°F oil or warm in the oven. Place refrigerated nuggets on a rack above a baking pan, and bake in a preheated 350°F oven for 5-7 minutes. For frozen nuggets, bake in 375°F oven for 20-25 minutes. Be sure to turn once while warming.

To Serve

Serve with Orange Honey Sauce (see page 90), Creamy Mustard Dip (see page 92), Pat Tung's Gourmet Delight Sweet-Sour Sauce, ketchup, or your favorite sauce.

Terrific Teriyaki

These crisp beef teriyaki sticks can be an appetizer or a main dish.

½ lb. flank steak

MARINADE
    2 tbsp. soy sauce
    1 tbsp. sherry
    1 tbsp. sugar
    1 clove garlic, crushed
    ½ tsp. chopped ginger root

2 cups cornflakes
Super Batter Mix
oil for frying

Preparation

1. Soak flank steak in cold water for 30 minutes to release blood. Rinse and pat dry.
2. Trim fat and membrane.
3. Cut steak cross-grain into ¾-inch strips. Cut long strips in half lengthwise. Cut thick pieces cross-grain into halves. Each piece is approximately ¾-inch wide, 2½-inches long and ¼-inch thick. Marinate steak overnight or up to two days in refrigerator. Turn over once so that both sides will be seasoned with marinade. When ready to cook, remove ginger and garlic. Place beef sticks on paper towel and blot dry.
4. Place cornflakes in a fold of waxed paper. Use rolling pin to crumble cornflakes, either coarse or fine, as desired.
5. Mix batter. Dip each piece of steak in batter first, and let excess batter drip off. Then roll in cornflake crumbs. (Steps 1-5 may be prepared ahead and the pieces refrigerated until cooking time.)

Cooking

Heat oil to 375°F. Fry six or seven pieces at a time till golden brown. Continue to fry the rest.

Note: Cut into ¾-inch pieces. The sticks can be served either hot or cold as an appetizer.

A Fifteen-Minute Complete Meal Plan

No time to cook? Here is the answer—a fast, simple, yet deliciously satisfying main dish. It can be prepared in four to five minutes. By working out a procedure, a complete meal for two can be served in fifteen minutes, for four in twenty minutes or less.

MENU
Soup (optional)
Baked Rolls
Fresh Salad
Fried Fish, Chicken, Pork, or Veal

Suggested Working Procedure

1. Place rolls in the oven if they require 8-12 minutes' baking time, and set timer. If rolls require 3-4 minutes to warm, then do it after step 4.
2. Warm canned soup (optional).
3. Heat oil for frying to low heat.
4. Mix Super Batter Mix.
5. Rinse fish fillet or meat, pat dry, dip in batter, and adjust heat to 375°F (medium high).
6. Test oil, then fry. While meat or fish is frying (approximately 2 minutes on each side), start to fix salad. When fish or meat is brown on one side, turn over and continue salad preparation.
7. Check soup. Remove fish or meat when both sides are golden brown. Remove rolls when ready.

Enjoy your meal!

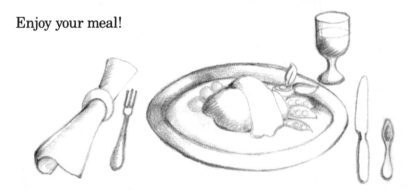

Fantastic Fish

Super Batter Mix is used on the catch of the day by many fishermen and campers. It is a perfect match to produce the ultimate in fried fish!

Super Batter Mix
1 lb. fish fillets, fresh or frozen (thawed)
oil for frying

Preparation

1. Mix batter.
2. Rinse fish fillets and pat dry. Cut long or large pieces into half.

Cooking

Heat oil to 375°F (medium high). Dip fish in batter, and let excess batter drip off. Deep-fry in oil till brown on one side (approximately 1½-2 minutes). Turn over. Remove when both sides are golden brown.

To Serve

- Serve with Pat Tung's Gourmet Delight Mustard Dipping Mix, Sweet-Sour Sauce or tartar sauce.

Note: If you prefer a coating, dip fish in cornflake crumbs, bread crumbs, almond slices, or sesame seeds before frying. You'll enjoy the contrast of textures.

Mrs. Hsu Chuan-Chen's Pork Tenderloin

This is my mother's favorite. I sent several packages of my products to my parents in Taipei, Taiwan. They say the quality and texture surpass any commercial batter products they have used. Here is one way they enjoyed using Super Batter Mix. Soy sauce gives it a salty flavor, and sherry is used to help to eliminate the "meat odor," a typical preparation step in Chinese cooking.

> 1 lb. pork tenderloin
> 2 tbsp. soy sauce
> 2 tbsp. sherry
> Super Batter Mix
> oil for frying

Preparation

1. Rinse pork and pat dry. Remove fat or membrane.
2. Slice pork into ¼-inch pieces. Pound gently with a mallet or the flat side of a knife. Marinate in soy sauce and sherry overnight (or 1-2 days in the refrigerator), so that the pork will absorb the seasoning. Place pork slices on paper towels and gently blot dry.
3. Mix batter.

Cooking

Heat oil to 375°F. Dip pork slices in batter and let excess batter drip off. Fry pork until both sides are golden brown.

Precious Veal

1 lb. veal scallopini or
  1½ lb. veal loin chops or rib chops (¾-1" thick)
1½ tbsp. soy sauce
2 tsp. sherry
1 cup cornflakes
¼ cup Pat Tung's Gourmet Delight Sesame Seeds
Super Batter Mix
oil for frying

Preparation

1. Rinse veal and pat dry. If veal pieces are large, cut in half. Remove bones from chops. Tenderize meat by pounding with a mallet until it is flat and ¼-inch thick. Marinate in soy sauce and sherry for a few hours. Before cooking, drain veal on paper towels and pat dry.
2. Roll cornflakes into crumbs and mix with sesame seeds in a dish. (May be done ahead of time, then covered.)
3. Mix batter.
4. Dip veal in batter and coat with mixture of cornflake crumbs and sesame seeds.

Cooking

Heat oil to 375°F. Fry two pieces at a time till brown, then turn over. Cook 2 minutes on each side. Remove when both sides are golden brown.

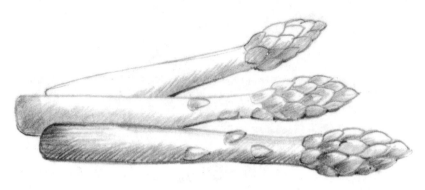

Asparagus

Clean 1 pound asparagus and trim off the stalk ends. Cut each stalk in half, dip in batter, and fry until golden brown.

Broccoli

Rinse broccoli, shake water off, and pat dry. Cut 1-inch below florets. Lightly dip florets in batter and let excess batter drip off. Fry in 375°F oil till florets are dark green, covered by light-brown batter.

Cauliflower

Cut cauliflower 1-inch below florets. Dip in batter and fry in 375°F oil till golden brown. Serve with various dips or chutneys, or sprinkle Parmesan cheese on top.

Eggplant

Rinse eggplant and pat dry. Slice into ¼-inch pieces. Dip in batter and fry in 375°F oil till golden brown.

Green Beans

Rinse beans and pat dry. Snip off both ends. Dip in batter and fry in 375°F oil till golden brown.

Mushrooms

Clean mushrooms and remove ¼-inch from stems, dip in batter, and fry at 375°F till golden brown. For easy serving, stick a toothpick into each mushroom.

The Best-Ever Onion Rings

1 lb. onions
Super Batter Mix
oil for frying

Preparation

1. Peel skin from onions. (Using refrigerated onions will eliminate tears.)
2. Cut onions crosswise into ¼-inch slices and separate into rings. (Rings may be prepared ahead and refrigerated.)
3. Mix batter.

Cooking

Heat oil to 375°-400°F. Dip onion rings in batter and let excess batter drip off. Fry until golden brown. Keep cooked onion rings warm in the oven on a rack above a pan, while continuing to fry the rest.

Note: You can use any variety of onion for this recipe. For sweeter taste, use Spanish onions.

Potatoes

Peel potatoes and cut into slices ¹⁄₁₆-⅛-inch. Dip in batter, let excess batter drip off, and fry in 375°F oil till golden brown.

Spinach

Clean spinach and pat dry. Tear each spinach leaf into 3 or 4 pieces. Dip in batter and let excess batter drip off. Fry in 375°-400°F till batter forms crust and becomes crisp.

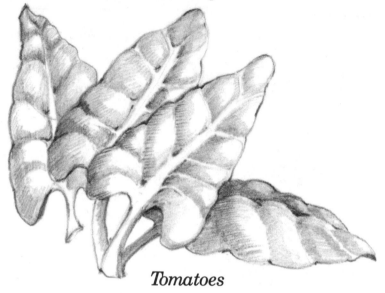

Tomatoes

Wash very, very firm or green tomatoes and pat dry. Cut each into ½-inch slices and roll lightly in flour. Dip in batter and let excess batter drip off. Fry in 375°F oil till golden brown. Serve with honey or sprinkle with sugar or Parmesan cheese.

Yams

Peel yams or sweet potatoes, cut into ⅛-inch slices. Dip in batter and let excess batter drip off. Fry in 375°F oil till golden brown.

Zucchini

Wash zucchini and pat dry. Cut each zucchini into finger-size sticks or ¼-inch slices. Dip in batter and let excess batter drip off. Fry in 375°F oil until both sides are golden brown. Serve with Parmesan cheese, Creamy Mustard Dip (see page 92), or creamy horseradish sauce.

Yummy Bananas

Super Batter Mix
4 bananas
oil for deep frying
powdered sugar
cinnamon or nutmeg
fudge sauce (optional)

Preparation

1. Mix batter.
2. Peel bananas and slice diagonally into ¼-inch pieces. Dip in batter and deep-fry at 375°-400°F. Turn when one side is brown (approximately 1-1½ minutes). Remove when both sides are golden brown. Sprinkle with powdered sugar and/or cinnamon or nutmeg. Or serve with fudge sauce.

Other Serving Suggestions

* *Frozen Fried Banana:* When cool, fried banana can be placed in freezer and later served frozen with fudge sauce.
* *Fried Banana Strawberry Ice Cream Sundae:* Place one scoop of vanilla ice cream in the center of a serving dish surrounded with five or six fried banana pieces to form petals. Pour strawberry topping over ice cream and serve.

43

Banana Supreme

Super Batter Mix
½ cup shredded coconut
¼ cup Pat Tung's Gourmet Delight Sesame Seeds
4-5 bananas
oil for frying
powdered sugar

Preparation

1. Mix batter.
2. Combine coconut shreds and sesame seeds in a dish.
3. Peel bananas and slice diagonally into ¼-inch pieces. Dip in batter, let batter drip off a little, then roll in mixture of coconut and sesame seeds. Deep-fry in 375°F oil, turning when one side is brown (approximately 1-1½ minutes). Remove when both sides are golden brown. Sprinkle with powdered sugar.

Apples Americana

To bake an apple pie takes fifty minutes. Why not take a fraction of the time to delight your friends and family with this treat?

> **4-5 apples**
> **Super Batter Mix**
> **oil for frying**
> **powdered sugar**
> **cinnamon**

Preparation

1. Wash and peel apples. Wedge-cut each apple into six to eight pieces, then cut off the core portion. Or you may core the apples first, then cross-cut them into ½-inch dough-nut-shaped slices.
2. Mix batter.

Cooking

Dip apple pieces in batter and fry in 375°-400°F oil till golden brown.

To Serve

• Blot fried apples dry with paper towel and sprinkle with powdered sugar and cinnamon. Or, if you prefer, garnish with fresh fruits or raisins and nuts.

Peachy Peaches

---

1 lb. firm peaches
Super Batter Mix
oil for frying
peach ice cream
peach brandy or peach liqueur (optional)

Preparation

1. Rinse peaches and pat dry. Remove skin if you wish. Cut peaches in wedges.
2. Mix batter.

Cooking

Heat oil to 375°F. Dip peach wedges in batter and deep-fry till golden brown.

To Serve

- Place five peach wedges around a scoop of peach ice cream and drizzle with peach brandy.

Nectarine Nibbler

1 lb. nectarines
Super Batter Mix
oil for frying
confectioner's or granulated sugar (optional)

Preparation

1. Rinse nectarines, pat dry, and remove skin. Cut nectarines into bite-size pieces.
2. Mix batter.

Cooking

Heat oil to 375°F. Dip nectarine pieces into batter and fry until golden brown. Sprinkle with sugar if you wish.

Fried Ice-Cream Sandwiches

ice-cream sandwiches
Super Batter Mix
oil for frying

Preparation

1. Set freezer at the coldest setting to store ice-cream sandwiches.
2. Mix batter.

Cooking

Heat oil to 400°F. Unwrap one ice-cream sandwich and cut it into two sections for easy handling when frying. Dip in batter and fry for 45-50 seconds while turning it over or basting it. Serve immediately. Continue to fry other ice-cream sandwiches.

3

Simple, Elegant Delectables for Special Occasions

**All uniquely appetizing,
and sure to delight every gourmet!**

Glorious Cheese

**1 lb. Cheddar, Colby, fontina, Gruyére, Monterey
Jack, or any hard cheese
Super Batter Mix
oil for deep-frying**

Preparation

1. Slice cheese into ¾-inch-wide strips, then cut each strip in half (each piece about ¾" × 2¾" × ⅝") or into cubes (¾" × 1"). Freeze cheese overnight or a few days in its original package; then wrap in foil until ready to fry.
2. Mix batter.

Cooking

Heat oil to 400°F. Dip frozen cheese (do not thaw) in batter and deep-fry until light brown, for only about 40-60 seconds. Fry four or five strips (or six to eight cubes) at a time. Do not overbrown, or cheese will leak from coating.

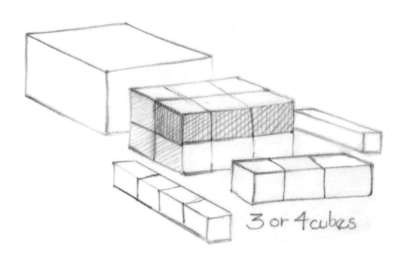

3 or 4 cubes

Jackie Barrett's Aristocratic Artichoke Hearts

A divine appetizer. Jackie Barrett is a chef at Marriott Hotel in Cleveland.

1 tsp. milk or half and half
3 oz. cream cheese
4 oz. crumbled blue cheese
2 cans artichoke hearts (16 artichoke hearts)
Super Batter Mix
oil for deep-frying

Preparation

1. Blend milk into cream cheese, then combine with blue cheese.
2. Drain artichoke hearts. Stuff cheese mixture in the center of each artichoke heart. (May be prepared ahead of time and refrigerated.)
3. Mix batter.

Cooking

Heat oil to 375°F and test for readiness. Dip artichoke heart in batter and deep-fry for 1½-2 minutes.

To Serve

• Cut artichoke hearts in half vertically. Place side by side on serving plate, cheese side up. Serve with mango chutney.

Note: Fried artichoke hearts without cheese filling are also divine.

Sensational Cheesy Mushrooms

The yellow yolk in the center of a halved hard-boiled egg inspired the choice of cheeses used here. The taste is sensational!

Super Batter Mix
3 oz. cream cheese
4 oz. shredded Cheddar cheese
12-16 oz. fresh mushrooms
oil for deep-frying

Preparation

1. Mix batter.
2. Combine cream cheese and Cheddar cheese.
3. Clean mushrooms and remove stems. Stuff caps with cheese mixture. (May be prepared ahead of time and refrigerated.)

Cooking

Heat oil to 375°F. Dip mushrooms in batter and deep-fry five or six at a time, making sure the cheese side is up to prevent cheese from leaking out. Use a long-handled spoon to baste the cheese side to seal the batter and cheese. When the cap is golden brown (approximately 1½-2 minutes), turn over and brown the other side for a short time (20-25 seconds).

To Serve

- Cut each large mushroom in half and serve with the cheese side up.

Note: For a party, you may serve raw cheese-stuffed mushrooms as well as batter-fried stuffed mushrooms. Arrange them either half and half on a plate, or arrange raw ones as the borders and freshly fried ones in the center.

John Saile's Zestful Zucchini Blossoms

John Saile is co-owner of the prestigious Heck's Cafe in Rocky River, Ohio, and Ohio City in Cleveland. This delightful dish can be a main dish as well as an appetizer.

3 oz. smoked salmon
8 oz. cream cheese

SEASONINGS
⅛ tsp. Pat Tung's Mustard Dipping Mix or
    any dried mustard
⅛ tsp. white pepper
pinch fresh thyme
¼ tsp. Worcestershire sauce
¼ tsp. lemon juice
¼ tsp. onion juice

16 freshly picked zucchini blossoms, pesticide-free
Super Batter Mix
peanut oil for frying

Preparation

1. Purée salmon in a blender or food processor. Then blend with cream cheese and seasonings.
2. Gently open the zucchini blossoms. Use a pastry tube to stuff salmon and cheese mixture in each blossom. Use your palm to close the blossoms by smoothing the opening.
3. Mix batter.

Cooking

Heat oil to 375°F. Dip stuffed blossoms in batter and deep-fry until crust turns golden brown.

To Serve

• As an appetizer, serve on a washed, pesticide-free zucchini leaf if you can get one from your garden.
• As a main dish, serve with pasta already tossed with cream, thyme, and grated fontinella cheese, along with a green salad.

Tasty Turkey Cheese Rolls

American cheese (individually wrapped slices)
Thin slices of turkey breast (available at
   delicatessens)
Super Batter Mix
oil for frying

Preparation

1. Put a piece of cheese on top of a turkey slice, making sure the turkey slice is larger than the cheese, so that cheese will be completely covered. Roll into a log or wrap over to cover cheese. If necessary, use toothpicks to fasten.
2. Mix batter.

Cooking

Heat oil to 375°F. Dip turkey-cheese roll in batter, then fry till golden brown. If you are deep-frying, do not remove toothpicks. If you are shallow-frying, carefully remove them before turning rolls over.

To Serve

- Serve on buttered toast with a salad dish.
- Serve as a main dish for lunch with a fruit salad.
- To serve as an appetizer, cut each roll into three or four sections.

Sonny Cloud's Coconut Scampi

Yum. . .m. . .m! Just superb! Sonny Cloud is the head chef at Sweet-water Cafe, Cleveland, Ohio.

1 lb. fresh raw scampi (16 count)
1 fresh pineapple
6 oz. mango or pineapple chutney
3 oz. white wine
Super Batter Mix
oil for frying
1 cup coconut flakes

Preparation

1. Shell scampi; leave the tail on. Butterfly scampi by cutting the back curved part open without cutting through. Devein, rinse, and pat dry.
2. Quarter pineapple lengthwise; core each quarter and separate pineapple from the outer skin, making sure to leave ½-inch on both ends; slice cross-length into seven pieces. Arrange the pieces on the skin so that the coconut scampi can sit on it with tails pointing up.
3. Purée chutney. Combine with wine.
4. Mix batter.

Cooking

1. Heat oil to 375°F, dip each scampi in batter, let excess batter drip off, then roll in coconut flakes. Fry scampi until both sides are golden brown (approximately 3 minutes).
2. Heat chutney and wine till warm. (Can be done ahead or simultaneously while frying scampi.)

To Serve

• Place scampi on pineapple slices. Top scampi with chutney-and-wine sauce.

Super Scallops

1 lb. fresh large sea scallops or bay scallops
1 tsp. baking soda
Super Batter Mix
oil for deep-frying

Preparation

1. Rinse scallops well. Slice each sea scallop horizontally into three thin pieces by making two layer cuts. Mix in baking soda and let stand for 30 minutes. Rinse well and pat dry.
2. Mix batter.

Cooking

Dip scallops in batter. If using tiny bay scallops, which are difficult to fry individually, use a toothpick to skewer two or three, but leave a little space in between. Deep-fry in 375°F oil until brown on one side. Turn over and fry until golden brown on other side.

To Serve

- Serve with your favorite sauce, Pat Tung's Gourmet Delight Mustard Dipping Mix, or Sweet Sour Sauce.

Sweet-Sour Chicken Or Pork

12-14 oz. chicken breast fillet (3-4 chicken breast halves) or pork tenderloin or loin
2 green or red sweet peppers
1 onion
10 cherry tomatoes
8 water chestnuts
1 can (8 oz.) pineapple chunks
Super Batter Mix

SWEET-SOUR SAUCE
  2 tbsp. cornstarch, dissolved in ½ cup
    plus 2 tbsp. water
  ½ cup sugar
  6 tbsp. vinegar
  ¼ cup ketchup
  4 tsp. soy sauce
  1 tsp. oil

oil for deep-frying

Preparation

1. Tenderize chicken or pork with a mallet or the flat side of a cleaver or knife. Cut into cubes (1" × 1").
2. Cube peppers and onion. Rinse tomatoes. Cut water chestnuts in half. Drain pineapple.
3. Mix batter.
4. Mix sweet-sour sauce.

Cooking

1. Heat oil to 375°F. Dip chicken (or pork) in batter and deep-fry until both sides turn golden brown (approximately 3-4 minutes). Remove chicken and place on a rack above a baking dish in the oven to keep warm. Continue to fry chicken pieces.
2. Add 3 tablespoons oil to a pan or wok. Stir-fry cubed pepper, onion, water chestnuts, tomatoes, and pineapple. Add sweet-sour sauce and stir until thickened.

To Serve

• Use the sauce as a dip for the chicken pieces or add it to the cooked meat, mix well, and serve immediately.

Meat Balls

1 lb. lean ground beef or veal
Super Batter Mix
oil for frying

Preparation

1. Divide ground meat into four portions (¼ pound each). Divide each portion into ten equal pieces, and roll each piece into a ball.
2. Mix batter.

Cooking

1. Heat oil to 375°F. Dip meatball into batter, and let excess batter drip off. Deep-fry eight at a time until golden brown.
2. Continue frying the rest, while warming the already fried meatballs on a rack above a pan in the oven.

To Serve

Pierce meatballs with cocktail picks and serve with any of the following:
- For Italian flavor: spaghetti sauce
- For French flavor: any creamy sauce
- For Oriental flavor: sweet-sour sauce
- For spicy flavor: hot sauce

Incredible Crepes

**any type of homemade filled crepes or
    Stouffer's Spinach Crepes
Super Batter Mix
oil for frying**

Preparation

1. Make and fill crepes according to your favorite recipe. If you use commercial frozen crepes, bake as directed and wait till completely cool (do this step ahead).
2. Mix batter in a dish that is long enough to cover the crepes, or else cut each crepe into half.

Cooking

Heat oil to 375°F. Dip crepes in batter. Transfer crepe to oil with a slotted spoon, and deep-fry until golden brown on both sides. If you prefer shallow frying, baste top part of crepe, and turn over when fried side is brown. Drain on paper towels and serve immediately.

Bea Delpapa's Chiles Rellenos De Queso
(Green Chilies filled with cheese)

Bea Allison Delpapa has traveled extensively in Mexico and New Mexico and has taught Mexican cooking for many years. She is the founder of Riverside Cooking School in Lakewood, Ohio.

7-9 chilies (either Poblano or Anaheim fresh or
**   canned whole green chilies)**
1 oz. Muenster or Monterey Jack cheese per chili
Super Batter Mix
1 egg (optional)
flour
oil for frying

Preparation

1. If using fresh chilies, wash well and place them directly over a flame or under the broiler. Let the skin blister and burn. Turn chilies from time to time so they do not get overcooked.
2. Place chilies in a paper or plastic bag, or wrap in a damp towel, and leave for about 10-20 minutes. The burned skin should peel or flake off easily. Peel and rinse.
3. Make a slit in the side of each chili and carefully remove the seeds and veins. Be careful to leave the top and the stem of the chili intact. (If the chilies are too spicy hot *(picante)*, let them soak in a very mild vinegar-and-water solution for about 30 minutes.) Rinse carefully.
4. Stuff chilies with cheese. Set aside.
5. Mix batter. If you wish you may add an egg for a flakier coating.
6. Pat chilies completely dry and dust them with a little flour.

Cooking

Coat chilies with batter and fry in hot oil, turning until they are golden all over. Drain on a rack over paper toweling and serve immediately with Tomato Salsa (see page 91).

Splendid Zucchini Stuffed With Caviar

Lip smacking treats!

1 lb. medium zucchini
1 jar (2 oz.) caviar, any variety
Super Batter Mix
oil for frying

Preparation

1. Rinse zucchini and pat dry. Cross-cut each zucchini into ½-inch slices.
2. Cut into slices to open a slit forming a pocket with ¼-inch on each side. Do not cut through the ends.
3. Scoop caviar with a small spoon and stuff it into each pocket. Smooth all edges so that caviar is closed in, not sticking out. (May be done ahead of time and refrigerated.)
4. Mix batter.

Cooking

Heat oil to 375°F. Dip each zucchini slice in batter and fry until golden brown on both sides.

To Serve

• If you have used more than one type of caviar, cut fried zucchini slices in half so that the different colors will show.

Mouth-Watering Soufflé

Mushrooms stuffed with spinach soufflé.

1 package (12 oz.) Stouffers' Spinach Soufflé
1 lb. mushrooms
Super Batter Mix
oil for frying

Preparation

1. Bake spinach soufflé according to directions on package. Let cool completely. (May be prepared the day before and refrigerated.)
2. Clean mushrooms and remove stems.
3. Fill each mushroom cap with spinach soufflé. Use a sandwich knife to smooth the edges for a neat appearance. (Preparation can be done ahead. Cover and refrigerate until ready to coat with batter and fry.)
4. Mix batter.

Cooking

Heat oil to 375°F. Dip mushrooms in batter and let excess batter drip off. Place mushrooms cap side down in the oil. Baste the spinach side. When cap side is brown (approximately 1½-2 minutes), turn over and continue to fry. Remove when both sides are golden brown.

Zona Spray's Fried Chèvre Cheese on Salad

Crispy fried goat cheese laid on top of a variety of salad greens, with a strawberry, a few fresh mushroom slices, and fresh herbs. Drizzle your favorite salad dressing over the top, preferably one made with a fruit vinegar. The result is a beautiful sight—not to mention the taste! Zona Spray operates her own cooking school in Hudson, Ohio. It has been considered the best between New York and Chicago, with visiting chefs and experienced teachers from around the world. She is also the proprietor of the Cookery, a gourmet specialty store adjacent to the school at 140 N. Main Street.

8 oz. Montrachet or Boucheron cheese
Super Batter Mix
4-5 different varieties of salad greens
6-8 large whole strawberries
fresh mushrooms, sliced
classic vinaigrette or favorite salad dressing
oil for deep frying

Preparation

1. Cut Montrachet into 1-inch pieces. If you use Boucheron, cut or mold it into 1-inch squares or rounds. Cover and freeze 1 hour or longer.
2. Mix batter.
3. Prepare salad, making individual plates of salad greens garnished with a strawberry and mushroom slices here and there. Sprinkle fresh herbs over all.

Cooking

Heat oil to 375°-400°F. Dip frozen cheese in batter and deep-fry six to eight pieces at a time till coating is formed and crisp (approximately 1-1½ minutes).

To Serve

• Lay fried cheese on top of the salad and serve immediately while hot with your favorite dressing.

Vegetable Trios

1 small zucchini
8 mushrooms
2 small onions
Super Batter Mix
oil for frying

Preparation

1. Scrub zucchini, rinse, and pat dry. Cube.
2. Clean mushrooms and pat dry.
3. Quarter onions.
4. Mix batter in a tall glass.
5. Use a 6-inch bamboo or stainless skewer or toothpick to skewer onion, then zucchini, and finally mushroom. Make sure to leave a small space between each piece.
6. Dip skewered vegetables in batter, and let excess drip off.

Cooking

Fry in 375°F oil for 3-4 minutes until brown.

Note:

- If pieces of food are packed too closely together, the batter between them may not be properly cooked.
- Vegetables may be marinated beforehand, but make sure you pat them dry before dipping them in batter.

John Zinitz's Fabulous Fried Strawberries or Pineapple

John Zinitz, a Northern Ohio chef, is presently with Top Services of Cleveland and operates a catering service in Rocky River.

Super Batter Mix
2 tsp. sugar
½ tsp. salt
½ tsp. baking powder
1 tbsp. Grand Marnier
¾ cup minus 1 tbsp. water
1 tbsp. corn oil
⅓ cup flour
⅓ cup cornstarch
1 pt. medium-size fresh strawberries, hulled, or
**   1 fresh pineapple cut into ½″ chunks**
2 cups corn oil for deep frying
powdered sugar

Preparation

1. Empty Super Batter Mix into a bowl. Add sugar, salt, baking powder, Grand Marnier, water, and 1 tablespoon corn oil. Stir until batter is blended.
2. Mix flour and cornstarch in a bowl. Dredge strawberries or pineapple chunks in flour-and-cornstarch mixture.

Cooking

1. Heat 2 cups corn oil to 375°F. Dip each strawberry or pineapple chunk in batter and deep-fry six to seven at a time until golden brown (approximately 1½ minutes).
2. Blot fried fruits dry and sprinkle with powdered sugar.

Flaming Banana

This recipe was inspired by Julia Ball of Rocky River, Ohio

Orange-Honey Sauce (see page 90)
Super Batter Mix
4 bananas
2 cups corn, peanut, or vegetable oil for deep frying
¼ cup rum (100 proof)

Preparation

1. Mix Orange-Honey Sauce.
2. Mix batter.
3. Peel bananas and cut each crosswise into five or six sections.

Cooking

1. Heat oil to 375°-400°F. Dip each banana section in batter and deep-fry until golden brown on both sides (approximately 2-3 minutes). Place fried bananas on a rack above a pan lined with foil so that the oil will drip through, then blot dry with a paper towel.
2. Transfer bananas to a heatproof plate, add heated rum, and ignite with a long match. When flame is diminished, pour Orange-Honey Sauce over bananas. Mix well and serve immediately.

Note: Bananas can be fried ahead of time till lightly browned. Re-fry before flaming. After igniting the dish, do not put your face near it. Keep a safe distance from the flame.

Party Pound Cake

pound cake
Super Batter Mix
oil for frying
ice cream

Preparation

1. Cut pound cake into ½-inch slices, and then halve each slice to make pieces about 1½" x 2".
2. Mix batter.

Cooking

Dip in batter and deep-fry at 375°-400°F till golden brown on both sides. Drain on paper towels.

To Serve

• Place two or three pieces of cake on a plate and top with ice cream. Add sauces or sprinkle with chopped nuts, or top with whipped cream and fresh or frozen fruit.

Fried Ice Cream

Is it possible to fry ice cream? Is it merely a joke? Or is it a novel approach to gastronomic ecstasy?

"Say what?" was the doubtful reaction from an eight-year-old neighbor when I once mentioned that I was going to serve him some fried ice cream. But among my adult friends, the immediate response to a hot, crisp coating over cold ice cream with a choice of mouth-watering toppings—colorful fresh fruits, whipped cream, sauces—has been unanimously enthusiastic.

The total frying time for ice cream is about 40-50 seconds in 400°F oil, or 1 minute in 375°F oil, but you must have everything ready—batter mixed, oil heated, garnishes and plates ready, and ice cream frozen solid.

This dessert must be served immediately after frying. For this, it will be good to have a helping hand in the kitchen. He or she can help add the toppings and garnishes and serve while you continue to fry the next one.

Caution: To ensure a perfect ice-cream dessert, buy ice cream that is frozen solid, preferably French or deluxe-type ice cream, and turn your freezer to the coldest setting to freeze your ice cream next to or near the ice trays.

Batter should coat the ice cream evenly, or else the ice cream may leak out, cloud the oil, and make sizzling sounds in the oil. Ask children to stay away from the stove, as you will be using high-temperature oil. Safety is very important.

Having observed these precautions, get ready for a fabulous treat!

Fried Ice Cream in Cake

1 angel food cake
ice cream of your choice
Super Batter Mix

GARNISHES
blueberries, strawberries, or raspberries
whipped cream

oil for frying

Preparation

1. Cut a piece of foil or two pieces of plastic wrap 9″ × 12″.
2. Cut angel food cake into four even sections. Either in the center of the foil or between pieces of plastic wrap, place the larger side (outer rim side) cake down, and roll each section to a flat piece approximately 6″ x 6″. Remove the top plastic wrap.
3. Place a 2-inch scoop of ice cream in the center of the cake. Bring the cake together to cover the ice cream by shaping the foil or plastic like a ball. Use a twist tie at the top to seal after making sure that the ice cream is fully covered by the cake.
4. Place in the freezer near the ice tray, at the coldest setting. (May be prepared days or weeks ahead.)
5. Mix batter in a 2-cup measuring cup or a deep bowl.
6. Have garnishes ready. Wash and clean berries and add sugar to them.

Cooking

Heat oil to 400°F. Unwrap an ice-cream ball. Dip in batter and fry till golden brown. If oil is shallow, baste the top with a long-handled spoon. When one side is brown, turn over. Remove when both sides are brown (approximately 1-1¼ minutes). Continue to fry the next one.

To Serve

• If serving 8, cut each piece in half. Garnish with whipped cream and pour berries over with syrup.

Waffle Wonders

Fried ice cream in waffles.

3 slices of ice cream
6 frozen waffles (each 4½″ × 3½″)
Super Batter Mix

GARNISHES
  cherry sauce (optional)
  1 pint strawberries, or other fresh fruits
    (optional)
  whipped cream

oil for deep-frying

Preparation

1. Sandwich one slice of ice cream in two pieces of waffle. Or spread a 2-inch scoop of ice cream evenly with a knife to within ¼-inch of edge of waffle. Press all edges of waffle firmly to seal. Wrap in foil and freeze until ready to deep-fry.
2. Mix batter in a dish large enough for waffle size.
3. Open a can of cherry sauce. Or prepare strawberry sauce by mixing 2 tablespoons sugar into a pint of berries and letting it stand.

Cooking

Heat oil to high. When temperature reaches 400°F, dip ice-cream sandwich in batter, making sure that batter covers the ice cream, and fry immediately in the hot oil. Use a long-handled spoon to baste. When one side is brown (approximately 20-25 seconds), turn over and fry for another 20-25 seconds. Remove. Continue to fry the next one.

To Serve

• Cut each fried ice-cream sandwich in half. Pour cherry or strawberry sauce over it, and top with whipped cream. Serve immediately.

Variations

- Spray whipped cream on top and garnish with fresh fruit (strawberries, bananas, kiwi slices, etc.).
- Use canned apple pie filling as a garnish.
- Use three giant-size waffles, each cut into two pieces, and adjust ice cream to approximate size, or spread a ½-inch scoop of ice cream evenly on top.

Note: Ice-cream slices come individually wrapped in cartons. Check the freezer case of your supermarket. You may, of course, slice brick ice cream yourself or use a 2-inch scoop of ice cream.

Fried Ice Cream In Cornflakes

corn flakes or frosted corn flakes cereal
ice cream (preferably French or deluxe)
fresh fruit and whipped cream (optional)
Super Batter Mix
oil for deep-frying

Preparation

1. Cut foil paper into 7-inch squares.
2. Break cornflakes into small pieces, but not crumbs.
3. Use ice-cream scoop to make 2-inch ice-cream balls. Roll each ball in cornflake pieces till fully covered. Wrap in foil and freeze individually until ready to use. (Can be prepared days ahead.)
4. Have fresh fruits cleaned and cut, ready for garnishing.
5. Mix Super Batter Mix in a 2-cup measuring cup, or any deep, narrow cup or dish large enough to dip ice cream in.
6. Have cooking utensils, serving plates, and garnishes ready.

Cooking

Heat oil to 400°F. Quickly unpack the frozen ice cream one at a time, dip in batter, and fry for 20-25 seconds. Use a long-handled spoon to baste the top. Turn over and fry the other side for another 20-25 seconds. Remove. Garnish with fresh fruits and whipped cream if desired. Serve immediately.

71

Icy Rice Krispies

Rice Krispies cereal
ice cream (preferably French or deluxe)
Super Batter Mix
fudge sauce
chopped nuts (walnuts, peanuts, pecans)
maraschino cherries
whipped cream (optional)
oil for deep-frying

Preparation

1. Cut foil paper into 7-inch squares.
2. Place Rice Krispies in a dish.
3. Use an ice-cream scoop to make a 2-inch ice cream ball. Roll it in Rice Krispies till fully covered, wrap it in foil, and freeze until ready to use. (Can be prepared days ahead and kept frozen.) Repeat to make more.
4. Mix Super Batter Mix in a 2-cup measuring cup or dish, or any dish large enough to dip the ice cream in.
5. Have cooking utensils, serving plates, fudge sauce, and other garnishes ready.

Cooking

Heat oil to 400°F. Quickly unpack the frozen ice cream one at a time, dip in batter, and fry for 20-25 seconds, basting with a long-handled spoon. Turn over and fry the other side for another 20-25 seconds. Remove, add fudge sauce, sprinkle on chopped nuts, and top with a maraschino cherry. Spray whipped cream around if desired. Serve immediately.

Chef Frank Waldron's Fried Ice Cream in Crepes

Sinfully delicious! Frank Waldron was the head chef at Lakewood Country Club when I first met him and supplied my Super Batter Mix to the club. It was after tasting his tantalizing creation that my interest in researching fried ice cream developed. Thank you, Frank!

> **French vanilla ice cream**
> **cinnamon**
> **sugar or brown sugar**
> **French crepes**
> **Super Batter Mix**
>
> **GARNISHES**
> **banana slices, strawberries**
>
> **oil for frying**
> **rum**

Preparation

1. Cut a section of ice cream (approximately 2″ × 3½″) big enough to be rolled in a crepe. Mix cinnamon and sugar in a dish and roll ice cream in it.
2. Roll ice cream in French crepe and wrap like an envelope. Wrap in foil and freeze at the coldest setting.
3. Mix batter.
4. Have garnishes ready.

Cooking

Heat oil to 375°F, dip frozen ice cream in batter, and deep-fry for 1 minute. Turn over and over while frying.

To Serve

- Place fried ice cream on a plate, garnish with slices of bananas and strawberries, and add a little rum on top. Serve immediately.

Fried Ice Cream In Almond Paste

Before President Ronald Reagan visited the People's Republic of China in April 1984, I read that the White House was deliberating over what to serve the President's hosts in China besides American turkey and California wine. This recipe was inspired by that news. Wouldn't it be a superlative treat for foreign heads and dignitaries to be served the best-quality American ice cream wrapped in an exquisite almond paste and fried in a light, crisp batter, topped with California fresh strawberries or Georgia peach slices? For all of us at home, the kings, queens, princes, and princesses of each household will certainly enjoy this royal treat.

> **1 can (8 oz.) pure almond paste or 1 tube (7 oz.)**
>   **almond paste**
> **ice cream (preferably French or deluxe), any flavor**
>
> **GARNISHES (optional)**
>   **Seasonal fruits (sliced)**
>   **whipped cream**
>   **almond slices or shredded toasted almonds**
>   **chocolate fudge sauce**
>
> **Super Batter Mix**
> **oil for frying**

Preparation

1. Cut almond paste into four even sections. Between two pieces of plastic wrap, roll each section into a thin piece (a 6-inch square or circle). Remove top sheet of wrap.
2. Cut ice cream into a slice 1″ x 1½″ x 3″. Envelope-wrap it inside the almond paste. Then wrap in plastic wrap or foil (use foil if prepared days ahead) and place near ice tray in freezer. Be sure to set freezer at coldest setting until ready to use. (May be prepared days or weeks ahead.) Continue to prepare the rest.
3. Prepare garnishes (optional).
4. Mix batter.

Cooking

Heat oil to 400°F. Have plate and garnishes ready. Take out ice-cream slices one at a time. Immediately dip in batter. To avoid messiness, use a slotted spoon to remove from batter and drop in oil to fry for 45-50 seconds till golden brown. Baste the top before turning over. If 375°F temperature is used, fry for 1 minute. Blot with paper towel, garnish, and serve at once. Continue to fry the next one.

4

Other Serving Ideas

From breakfast to parties—
won't you give these innovative
recipes a try?

BREAKFAST

Are you tired of eating the same breakfast foods all the time? Try these tempting variations, fried in a regular skillet with ½-inch oil.

Suggested Menu

Fruit Juices
Bacon Curls
Fried Waffles, Crispy English Muffins, or Fried Bread
Milk or Coffee

Fried Waffles

Instead of popping frozen waffles into the toaster, why not fry them in Super Batter Mix for a change?

Preparation

Cut thawed waffles into halves or quarters. Dip in batter and fry in 375°F oil until both sides are brown and crisp. Drain on paper towels.

To Serve

- Serve with heated blueberry or cherry sauce topped with whipped cream, maple syrup, whipped honey with margarine or butter, powdered sugar, or jam.

Crispy English Muffins

Cut English muffin halves into quarters. Dip in batter and fry until brown. Drain on paper towels. Serve with margarine or butter and jam or syrup.

78

Fried Bread

---

any variety of bread (white, wheat, potato, cinnamon, raisin, etc.)
Super Batter Mix
oil for frying
1 can apple pie filling
whipped cream

Preparation

1. Cut each piece of bread in half, either across or diagonally.
2. Mix batter.

Cooking

1. Heat oil to 375°-400°F. Dip bread pieces in batter, and let excess drip off. Fry until golden brown. Keep fried bread warm on a rack above a pan in a warm oven while continuing to fry the second and third batches.
2. Warm pie filling in a saucepan.

To Serve

• Place two pieces of fried bread (cut in half again, if you wish) on a plate. Top with warm pie filling and whipped cream.

Brunch

John Sime's Stuffed French Toast

A scrumptious eye-opener. John Simes is head chef at Heck's Cafe in Rocky River, Ohio.

1 cup fresh blueberries
1 tbsp. sugar
1 egg yolk
2 cups ricotta cheese
⅓-½ loaf French bread
Super Batter Mix
oil for frying

Preparation

1. Blend blueberries, sugar, egg yolk, and ricotta cheese. Refrigerate until approximately the consistency of cottage cheese. (May be prepared ahead of time.)
2. Slice French bread into 1½-inch pieces. Make a pocket in the center of the crust side, leaving ¼-inch on sides intact.
3. Stuff blueberry-cheese mixture into pocket of each slice of French bread. Smooth edges with a sandwich knife. (May be prepared ahead of time and refrigerated till ready to cook.)
4. Mix batter.

Cooking

Heat oil (2-inches deep) to 375°F. Dip each piece of bread in batter and let excess batter drip off. Fry until one side is brown, then turn over and brown the other side.

Serve with

- John Saile's Butterscotch Syrup (see page 90)
- Savory and sage pork sausage
- Mimosa (champagne and orange juice)

Lunch

Deep-Fried Hot Dogs

Have you ever tried a "corn dog" or "pronto pop"? It is a frankfurter on a stick covered with a cornmeal batter and deep-fried till golden brown, often dipped in mustard or ketchup to serve. In my version of this popular food, the good old familiar hot dogs taste great with a light, crisp Super Batter Mix coating. This recipe is a welcome change that will delight kids of all ages.

1 lb. hot dogs (any type)
bread crumbs (optional)
Super Batter Mix
oil for frying

Preparation

1. Thaw hot dogs if frozen and pat dry. If preparing this recipe is a spur-of-the-moment idea, cook frozen hot dogs in water, drain and pat dry. Roll in bread crumbs if desired.
2. Mix batter.

Cooking

Dip hot dogs in batter and deep-fry until golden brown, approximately 2 minutes on each side. Drain on paper towels. Put a stick into each hot dog if you wish. Sticks may be placed in hot dogs before frying, but then you will need a deep fryer, so that the hot dogs may be fried vertically.

To Serve

- Serve with mustard and ketchup.

Mashed Potato and Tuna Patties

leftover mashed potatoes
canned tuna
bread crumbs
Super Batter Mix
oil for frying

Preparation

Mix each ½ cup leftover mashed potatoes with one-fourth of a 7-ounce can of tuna. Add 2-3 tablespoons bread crumbs. (Add more bread crumbs if the mixture is too soft to handle.) Roll into 1½-inch balls or flatten into patties.

Cooking

Dip in batter and fry in 375°F oil till golden brown.

Snack

Sunflower Seed Fritters

½ packet Super Batter Mix
raw sunflower seeds
oil for frying

Preparation

1. Mix ½ cup Super Batter Mix with 6 tablespoons water and 1½ teaspoons oil.
2. Add sunflower seeds to batter.

Cooking

Heat oil to 375°F. Drop a teaspoonful of sunflower-seed batter into the oil. Fry six to eight spoonfuls at one time. Remove when they turn golden brown (approximately 1-1½ minutes).

Precooked Foods

If you have a microwave oven, you can use it to thaw frozen food quickly and then prepare it for batter-frying. Frozen cooked chicken and turkey, for example, can be cut into chunks or cubed and dipped into batter and fried.

Cold-Cut Meat Roll

Roll slices of roast beef, corned beef, or ham into logs. Cut each log into 1½-inch sections. Dip in batter and fry at 375°F till golden brown.

Roast Beef With Smoked Clams

These rolls can be served as an appetizer.

Roll each roast beef slice into a log, and cut into 1½-inch sections. Unroll each section, place two or three smoked clams inside, and then reroll to wrap clams. Dip in batter and fry till golden brown.

Leftovers

Leftovers are always a problem. You don't want to waste them, yet they are no longer appetizing. After a food has been reheated, the texture, flavor, and appearance are all deteriorated to a certain extent. But when cold leftovers are fried with a Super Batter coating, they take on a new life. You'll be amazed with the results.

Fried Pizza

Cut pizza into bite-size pieces. Dip in batter. Fry at 375°F till both sides are brown.

Meat and Poultry

Dice or slice cooked meat or poultry or cut into chunks. Dip in batter and fry at 375°F till golden brown on both sides. Serve with mustard sauce, barbecue sauce, sweet-sour sauce, honey sauce, or creamy mushroom sauce.

Summertime Quickies

Harry Truman's famous saying "If you can't stand the heat, get out of the kitchen" is not always literally possible. Unlike the political scene, in a domestic setting we have to cook despite the summertime heat. One way to shorten cooking time in front of the heat is to make batter-fried kabobs. You'll find it easy and fun for the family to skewer their own favorites, then dip in batter, and fry. (You can also dip food in batter before skewering.)

Suggested Menu

Chilled Fruit Salad
Fresh Corn
Seafood Kabobs with Dipping Sauce
Ice Cream or Sherbet

Caesar Salad
Fresh Corn
Seafood, Chicken and Vegetable Kabobs
Chocolate Eclairs or Cream Puffs

Seafood Kabobs

½ tsp. baking soda
½ lb. scallops
½ lb. fresh shrimp
½ lb. oysters
Super Batter Mix
oil for frying

Preparation

1. Sprinkle ½ teaspoon baking soda on scallops to tenderize. Mix well and let stand for 30 minutes. Rinse and pat dry.
2. Shell shrimp, devein, and pat dry.
3. Rinse oysters and pat dry.
4. Mix batter. If food is to be dipped in batter after being put on skewers, be sure to mix batter in a tall glass.

5. Thread each piece on a bamboo or stainless skewer (Make sure to leave a little space in between the pieces so that the food as well as the batter will be fully cooked). Dip seafood in batter and let excess batter drip off.

Cooking

Fry at 375°F. If the skewers are in a horizontal position during frying, be sure to turn them over. Remove when both sides are brown.

To Serve

• Serve with hot sauce or your favorite dips.

Chicken and Vegetable Kabobs

chicken breast fillet
zucchini
small onions
Super Batter Mix
oil for frying

Preparation

1. Cut chicken into cubes (1" × ¾" × 1").
2. Scrub zucchini, rinse, and pat dry. Cut into cubes the same size as chicken cubes.
3. Quarter onions.
4. Blend Super Batter Mix in a tall glass if food is to be skewered first. Skewer chicken cubes alternately with zucchini and onions. (Be sure to leave space between each piece.) Dip in batter. (An alternate method is to coat each piece in batter, let excess batter drip off, then skewer. This way the food will be fully coated, although your hands will get a bit messy.)

Cooking

Heat oil to 375°F in a utensil large enough to hold the kabob in a vertical or horizontal position. Deep-fry until golden brown.

85

Wintertime Fun

Fish and Chicken Fry Party for 6 to 12

Suggested Menu

Appetizer (Prepare ahead.)
Salad Bar (Prepare ahead.)
Fried Fish or Chicken, or Fried Kabobs
(Rinse and pat dry, then refrigerate.)
Baked Potato (Optional; prepare ahead.)
Dessert (Prepare ahead.)

Setup

- Arrange drinks and nibbles on one table.
- Put Salad Bar in center of another table.
- Place one or two deep-fryers (or electric woks, electric skillets or fondue skillets) containing oil for frying on a separate table.
- Have one or two persons in charge of cooking, or let guests do their own cooking. Guests can select their choice of food and have it cooked either in whole pieces or in kabob form.

Salad Bar Suggestions

applesauce
canned peaches
fresh fruits
macaroni salad
potato salad
three-bean salad
green onions
lettuce
beets
tomato slices or cherry tomatoes
broccoli
cauliflower
cucumber slices
mushrooms

salad dressings, Pat Tung's Gourmet Delight Mustard
   Dipping Mix or Sweet-Sour Sauce
croutons
bacon bits

Fish and Chicken Fry Ingredients:
Chicken (Layer-cut each chicken breast half
into two even pieces.)

Fish (Boneless fillet; cut large one in half.)

Kabob Ingredients
chicken (cubed)
pork (cubed)
beef (cubed)
fish
scallops (Tenderize first.)
shrimp (deveined and butterflied)
mushrooms (Remove stems.)
onions
zucchini (cubed)
green or red sweet peppers (cubed)

Other Items
Super Batter Mix (Can be prepared ahead and
refrigerated.)
Dipping sauces (Can be prepared ahead.)
oil
napkins
tongs
strainers
rack over a foil-lined pan
skewers

5
Dips And Sauces

Sauces And Dips

Tangy Apricot Sauce

Mix ½ cup apricot preserves
     1 tbsp. water
     1½ tsp. cider vinegar
     ½ tsp. ketchup

Orange-Honey Sauce

Mix ½ cup honey
     3 tbsp. frozen concentrated orange juice
     1 tbsp. water

John Saile's Butterscotch Syrup

½ lb. butter (slightly salted)
1 cup brown sugar
1½ cups pure maple syrup
1½ oz. Scotch whiskey

Preparation

In a saucepan, heat butter, brown sugar, and syrup until
syrup becomes bubbly. Stir to blend sugar well. Add Scotch
to the bubbly syrup and continue to cook for 15-20 seconds. Serve warm.

Bea Delpapa's Tomato Salsa

1 or 2 jalapeños (pickled)
1 small clove garlic
1 tbsp. jalapeño oil
1 can (16 oz.) tomatoes
½ tsp. cumin powder (cumino or cominos)
½ tsp. salt

Preparation

Place the jalapeños and garlic in blender or food processor and pulse off and on until roughly chopped. Add the rest of ingredients and pulse again. The sauce should not be completely smooth. If it is allowed to sit for a few hours, the flavors will blend more completely. This sauce can be heated and served over such dishes as chiles rellenos or served cold as a dip.

Oriental Soy-Sherry Dip

Mix 1 tbsp. soy sauce
1 tbsp. sherry
½ tbsp. water
1 tsp. sugar
⅛ tsp. black pepper

If hot and spicy flavor is desired, add hot sauce.

Oriental Soy-Vinegar Dip

Mix 1 tbsp. soy sauce
1 tbsp. water
1½ tbsp. vinegar

If hot and spicy flavor is desired, add hot sauce.

Hot and Spicy Mustard Dip

**Blend 1 tbsp. Pat Tung's Gourmet Delight Mustard
Dipping Mix
1 tbsp. cider vinegar
½ tsp. vegetable oil**

Let stand for 15 minutes. Ideal for batter-fried foods, egg rolls,
sashimi (Japanese raw fish), roast beef, ham, kielbasa (Polish sausage), and hamburgers.

Hot and Sweet Mustard Dip

**Blend 1 tbsp. Pat Tung's Gourmet Delight Mustard
Dipping Mix
1 tbsp. cider vinegar
½ tsp. vegetable oil
2 tsp. honey**

Creamy Mustard Dip

**Blend ½-3 tbsp. Pat Tung's Gourmet Delight Mustard
Dipping Mix
¼ cup vegetable oil
3 tbsp. cider vinegar
¼ tsp. salt
½ cup (4 oz.) sour cream**

Artichoke Blue-Cheese Dip

Blend 4 artichoke hearts (canned)
3 tbsp. artichoke juice (liquid in can)
1 tbsp. milk
½ cup crumbled blue cheese
1½ tsp. Pat Tung's Gourmet Delight Mustard
Dipping Mix

Mustard Vinaigrette Dressing

Blend 1 tsp. Pat Tung's Gourmet Delight Mustard Dipping
Mix
⅛ tsp. salt
⅓ cup vegetable oil (or half vegetable and half olive
oil)
¼ tsp. black pepper
¼ tsp. onion powder
3 tbsp. cider vinegar

Yogurt Mustard Dip or Dressing

Blend 1 cup plain yogurt
1-2 tbsp. Pat Tung's Gourmet Delight Mustard
Dipping Mix
½ tsp. salt

PAT TUNG'S GOURMET DELIGHT products are available in many gourmet and specialty food stores. If unavailable in your area, orders can be made by mail. Please send money order or check to:

**PAT TUNG'S INTERNATIONAL GOURMET, INC.,
Dept. M
P.O. Box 16141
Rocky River, Ohio 44116**

Item	Unit Price	Quantity	Total
Fried Ice Cream and Other Gourmet Delights (book)	$6.95		
Ohio residents add 6½% tax	0.46		
Postage and handling	1.25		
(If also ordering products, omit $1.25 handling charge)			
10 packets Super Batter Mix (All-Purpose)	19.90		
Postage and handling	2.50		

TOTAL _____

PAT TUNG'S GOURMET DELIGHT products are available in many gourmet and specialty food stores. If unavailable in your area, orders can be made by mail. Please send money order or check to:

PAT TUNG'S INTERNATIONAL GOURMET, INC.,
Dept. M
P.O. Box 16141
Rocky River, Ohio 44116

Item	Unit Price	Quantity	Total
Fried Ice Cream and Other Gourmet Delights (book)	$6.95		
Ohio residents add 6½% tax	0.46		
Postage and handling	1.25		
(If also ordering products, omit $1.25 handling charge)			
10 packets Super Batter Mix (All-Purpose)	19.90		
Postage and handling	2.50		
TOTAL			

(Please allow 6-8 weeks for delivery.
All prices are subject to change without notice)

(Please print or type)

Name_____

Address_____

City_____State_____Zip_____

☐ Please send me the institutional and professional list (for caterers, restaurants, and institutions only).

☐ For gift, please ship directly to:

Name_____

Address_____

City_____State_____Zip_____

Reorder Additional Copies